INSTINCTS

A Collection of Poems

AF107599

DR. RAJESH CHAUHAN

BlueRose ONE.com
Stories Matter
NewDelhi • London

BLUEROSE PUBLISHERS
India | U.K.

BlueRose ONE.com
Stories Matter
NewDelhi • London

For permissions requests or inquiries regarding this publication, please contact:

BLUEROSE PUBLISHERS
www.BlueRoseONE.com
info@bluerosepublishers.com
+91 8882 898 898
+4407342408967

ISBN: 978-93-6452-418-6

Cover design: Shivam
First Edition 2023
Second Edition: October 2024

I dedicate this work, *Instincts: A Collection of Poems,* in the memory of my mother, *Late Mrs. Krishna Kumari.* "Your memories will remain etched in our minds, eternally"! To my father, Mr. Balwant Singh who at ninety-five continues to shower his blessings and guide us!

"To save our world, we have to replace carbon prints with clean energy. Leaving our selfish interest aside, every nation should fully cooperate; otherwise our doom is not far away."

Dr. RP Agarwal

Paediatrician and Rotarian, Mumbai

"Adopting sustainable lifestyle choices is the way to reduce carbon emissions."

Vishakha Chauhan

Engineering Group Manager and DEI Ambassador @ site, Alstom Transportation, Mannheim

Contents

Preface

The very purpose of writing preface is to make readers aware of subtle details in the poetries as they roll over pages. These have been written instinctively from personal experiences with a hope that adjustment of lifestyles would make this world more beautiful to live in. As a practicing anesthesiologist, I consider it my obligation to present the message to the readers in an interesting way to mould their thought processes to seek their contribution in preserving nature through self corrective ways. Issues due to ego, power, and the quest to gain overall control on the landmass by the invaders working in tandem with traitors, enslaved the ethnic residents, brutally assaulted and looted for nearly a thousand years! Spiritual growth in the medieval periods followed with scriptures written by legendary writers and an era of dependence on supernatural forces to seek solace began in earnest way. These were labeled to be myths derived from "mythos" a Greek word, a term given by invaders to dilute the history of the nation, many have even begun thinking so, which is very unfortunate and denigrating our own values and ethos. History as a result clearly began being manipulated and many critical historical important events were ignored, side-lined and undue importance given to details since gaining independence, apparently to gain popular support and make the society appear more secular. Unread details began to mislead the coming generations, unjustified but true!

We are living in a restless world with endless problems. A flare and confusion could easily ignite the onset of third world war which could annihilate life on earth with likely use of nuclear weapons available in plenty. Can we afford a holocaust that brought an end to the Second World War, to be the starting point of another World War? A likely use of nuclear devices would be the most undesirable thing the world needs at this point when more vital issues connected with uncertainties due to climate change have yet to be resolved.

Problems of extremism and barbarism, being frequently shown on television, have been badly impacting the young minds and false portrayal of our history alone hasn't helped matters. The rich cultural heritage we have inherited with teachings of legendary writers and saints in the medieval era can guide people to adopt healthier lifestyles to promote personal intellectual and spiritual growth.

India famously known as "Bharat or Bharatvarsha" after legendary King "Bharata" was extending much beyond its current boundary and has been ruled by rulers with a number of small and large kingdoms, and at one time for a brief period under the rule of great Mauryan ruler, Aśoka, it was one huge land mass who ruled it with a firm hand, took to Buddhism at the end of Kalinga war spreading it across the world. The war had resulted in horrific killings on one single day, made residents to follow the dictum of not electing war to solve problems, as the tragic stories continued to be narrated for generations, an apparently weaker stance taught from a very tender age nevertheless social and sane all the same. The national emblem is a modification of lion of Sarnath, a sign of rich cultural heritage we have envisaged!

The climate change has been happening since the end of ice- age but is being increasingly felt in the recent years. Subtle monitoring and comparisons of vital parameters over time has made it possible to note change occurring in climate and is bring recorded objectively. The rapidly rising greenhouse gases, global warming, unseasonal rains, frequent cloudbursts, floods, and cyclones around the world, have started creating havoc with huge loss of lives and properties right across the globe. Periods of drought and flooding has caused strife with hunger related deaths globally.

Congested cities, wayward construction, migration of people in search of a better life, have compounded problems, with no easy solutions. There has been a shortage of space, scarcity of clean water and increasingly polluted air, proving to be a health hazard causing innumerable deaths. We can find all such issues in the cities we live in with improper disposal of garbage, creating hillocks of dumps waiting for proper disposal, should itself bring a sense of responsibility amongst inhabitants, to make serious attempt to remove indiscretion and in corrections, a top priority of each and every individual to make the cities beautiful, streets safe with facilities to make lives enjoyable where fragrance around abounds. The true strength of power should be analysed not by the number of wars won and nation's hegemony in the region or right across the world but it lies in waging war against climate change brought out by the activities of the man! Achieving this won't be easy as this would entail eternal peace, progressive and healthy competitions amongst nations globally, a wishful but achievable goal.

Plethora of memories has aroused the poet in me that has let me pen down poetries at leisure presented in subtle form in the collection, "Instincts *A Collection of Poems*". This envisage personal experiences, struggles - a part of life, being aware of "Perils all over", thought processes that goes to counter them, 'the "Never give up" attitude' while giving fair chance to individuals to succeed in life, all while reminiscing events in life. I am sure the readers would find it interesting as they keep rolling pages. As a student of science, I consider the thoughts that have encouraged me to write these poems have come to me as 'photons of energy' from the universe successfully trapped by penning them down before these could get erased from the mind, diluted by continuous flow of information trickling into the mind!

Signing off with, "Supreme God Shri Krishn", a poetic marvel trapped in a whirlpool of the "Phenomenon of success and failure", an ever pervading truth!

Dr. Rajesh Chauhan
MD Anaesthesia
New Delhi
April 5, 2023

Acknowledgements

Acknowledging the valuable help rendered while completing this book, *"Instincts: A Collection of Poems"*, I extend my sincere gratitude to my wife, Vibha and ever so grateful to my children - Vishakha, her husband Daniel Llin Ferrero, Hima, Devansh for their support, despite taking away their valuable time, as I continued to pen down my instincts in the form of poems. I am indebted to my father, Balwant Singh, who at ninety-five is going strong and keeps us engaged with advice on worldly matters! I have been fortunate to have had him by my side, listening to his experiences and opinions as he continued watching TV programmes while I continued tapping poems on my mobile, gaining new insights.

"We are running the most dangerous experiment in history right now, which is to see how much carbon dioxide the atmosphere can handle before there is an environmental catastrophe."

Elon Musk, CEO of Tesla & SpaceX

"Three decades ago when we were in school we were taught that climate change was going to cause global catastrophe in the next century or so..... fast forward to the present and the many cyclones, freak weather events, landslides, cloudbursts, desert floods and extreme heat waves make it feel that a century is already over...... the said catastrophe won't befall us suddenly, like in a Hollywood movie, it's going to creep up on us insidiously before we know it. It has started happening"

Dr. Anirban Kundu

Cardiac Surgeon, New Delhi.

Foreword

The poetry book, "Instincts: A Collection of Poems", by Dr. Rajesh Chauhan is a set of amazing poems covering a wide area of human activities he has brought to the fore, the extreme climate change its fallout. He has quite exquisitely informed through poems the scientific miscalculations in the last 200 years since industrialisation, been the primary reason for its change. The increased carbon load due to these activities has resulted in global warming with melting of glaciers and rising ocean level. This change is likely to affect life on earth and marine life in not too distant time say within couple of decades.

Reaching to his avid readers with a warning on reasons of the beginning of sixth mass extinction of life on earth with 40% loss of marine life that has already taken place as a subtle message in his poems seems an unbelievable effort. He naturally ends up advising them to spread the message to people to make changes in their life style which need to be in consonance with the nature otherwise it has in its garb such force, which if it unleashes, so huge would be its fury that it would remove the cause of change, the man, to set its own rule. He points out that the mismanagement by the man, busy in setting up his rule, is besieged with problems will be taken care of by nature interfering with his very survival. These are reflected in poems: "Perils on, Nature at War", "Nature's Devastation", "and Nature Change Now Constant".

The layout of the city being developed as in the West with fault lines has also affected, "The Capital City We Live in" and at length deals with factors affecting Delhi city overflowing with population. This has already adversely affected air, water and land with unprecedented pollution all over the city, rated to be the most polluted city in the World. Then there are poems dealing with successful people and those who fail in the, "Phenomenon of success and failure" in a free flowing train of thoughts richly experienced in life. Then the description on circle of life, "As Time Goes By", and a beautiful rendition on "Sky", "Intuition: The Sixth Sense" are very informative "Theo-philosophical" description that have come in his poems.

I sincerely hope that this book with collection of poems dealing on immensely important topics deserves wide circulation so that people learn to take measures to delay climate change, failing which, life may cease on earth much before it should. Measures like preventing wars, not helping matters either, have to be ensured to be able to safely say 'no more', "It's Yesterday Once More" written on World War II that has led to destruction of two cities in Japan and massacre of humanity all over the world! The third World War, if it takes place, may finish off in the first hour itself in case nuclear button gets switched on, as only a small population may be left by then which also would perish in due course of time!

I extend my best wishes to the author for the success of this book, as the cover picture of the book itself depicts the horror very likely to be faced in near future across the World. Unless everyone is in sync with the problem faced by humanity and that steps are taken to retrace steps on lead causes of climate change, we shall not be able to live safely on the only "Blue planet" in the Universe known till date which should be the place to keep safe and continue to live in. Otherwise, only course left would be to find another planet in "Sky" several light years away where only handful of people could migrate and the rest left to die on earth. Survival on the new planet would be like that of early man on Earth and imaginably not going to be easy. Unless effective steps are taken on an emergency basis a number of coastal cities that control World economics are likely to get submerged with rising ocean levels along with other factors is likely to annihilate life on earth. "Man being the weakest amongst the living beings stands being wiped out the earliest from the face of earth despite being the most intelligent amongst beings". May you continue to find motivation to write more and reflect on life experiences!

Dr. Naveen Saraf,
MS, MCh
New Delhi

"World population that stood at 1.6 billion in 1900 CE to 8.2 billion by mid-2024 CE, a 5-fold increase along with ease of lifestyle bestowed by science has led to massive increase in carbon emissions. This has to be controlled and demands decreased. It seems policy failure globally."

Dr. Rajesh Chauhan

Cardiac Anaesthesiologist and Author of Poem books "My Nature My World" and "Instincts A Collection of Poems"

"Climate change poses an existential threat to humanity, caused by human activities releasing greenhouse gases that lead to devastating consequences such as rising sea levels, intense natural disasters, and severe droughts. To mitigate this crisis, collective action is imperative, requiring immediate transitions to renewable energy, sustainable practices, and responsible policies to protect the planet's fragile ecosystem for future generations."

Dr HS Bedi

Cardiovascular Surgeon, Mohali.

1

As Time Goes By

Soul ever remains young, hunting experiences;
Travels through multiple lifetimes spent,
Gains timeless experiences, learning's:
Appearances change with time,
The change so happened,
Time has gone by!

Thinking of an era gone by,
Even multiplies with time,
Experiences-maturing with time,
The outlook simply modifies,
Entangles convictions, impressions!
As time passes by!

Remember the past,
Roll the clock back in time,
Refreshing memories once again!
Find things are not the same!
The changes now remarkable,
As the time passes by!

The days that were pink, appear grey.
As memory ink fades with time,
For the things do not remain the same,
As the time goes by!

The time is never the same,
As it goes by, so subtle is the change;
Changes noticed after a while,
Despite thoughts remaining young,
The changes now confirmed,
The loss of time so felt,
As the time goes by!

When aging happens,
Compare remembrances afresh,
As time moves away from past,
The time has passed by,
The process makes one older and wiser,
With mature thoughts taking over,
Nature's protection, call it God's safety device!
As the time passes by!

Of the spring, summer, and autumn of life;
As the winter of life gives a close call,
With time no longer in control,
Wait for time to shred the life,
As the soul renews itself, forever young it stays.
Over and again as it keeps coming afresh!
Life repeats somewhere,
As one completes the circle of life!
Young soul gets old,
Matures with time;
Transcendent state away from the cycle of rebirth!

2

Intuition: The Sixth Sense

Whatever is not seen?
Is not visible!
Whatever that is not visible,
Cannot be understood!
Whatever that is not understood,
Can be misunderstood!
Misunderstood can always be proven wrong!

Nothing is absolute in this World,
The social order of the day is important!
Prevails and hangs as a pendulum,
Moves between core truth and absolute fiction,
Trapped between truths and believing to be true,
Absolute lie is same as absolutely fictional,
Then, what is the key to right and wrong?

When vision and mind, misconnect;
Fact and fiction disconnect,
All that prevails is also not real,
Spontaneous mind-wandering attenuated viewing,
Vision and mind frequently off-track,
Free from constraints and intentions!
A normal variation to maintain mental balance!

It's exaggerated in abnormal mental states!
A thinking mind controls,
Correlation of vision and mind!
Is all that's required?
Where lays its correction?
Hearsay or having heard, is that real?
Not the least, not the least!
Seeing with eyes, is it right?
Not always, not always!

Intuition: the sixth sense – a hidden perception!
A connection of heart, soul, and mind!
When eyes, ears coordinate with intuition;
That Sixth Sense,
Is just enough to know it all!

3

Phenomenon of Success and Failure

When success begins to ride the head,
Beginning of failure starts setting in,
Fear of failure starts filling their head.

But of those wanting to succeed,
Appetite to succeed, excitement in deeds;
Soars, and gets the best out of them!

Degree of fullness is what that matters!
Desire to perform with space so empty,
Pockets of desires empty belief takes up the reins.

Fills the space with success and succeed.
Most successful with pockets of desire full,
Oh dear! What then happens to those at peak?

Flattened World and flattening of the curve they see,
Reaching the zenith, the fall could be free;
Feeling of fear to fail rides their head.

What is then the difference between the two?
Of the successful and those waiting to succeed,
Fluctuating resolve of wanting to succeed, fear of losing!

The way of thinking of the two,
One so positive, other getting negative;
Results so immense, carves their future.

At the peak, start looking down upon others;
In order to stay at peak, starts manipulating others; Fail to recognize those destined to succeed.

Less successful avails the opportunity,
Write success stories of many and succeed!
Both tread the common path.

Failure to be immensely successful,
Flying Sky high, down to bottom;
For nothing succeeds like success!

Surely, nothing fails like failure too;
Peaks and troughs stay for a period!
Many fail to note of those destined to succeed.

When dogs start barking,
An elephant was seen passing by;
Such is the story of the successful!

4

A Thought

Literature is a thought, written or verbal;
Thoughts indicate perspectives,
Texts of past becomes history,
Historical facts make traditions,
Traditions changes with time,
Time passes by!

Text perpetuates and grows,
Literature abounds and spreads,
Unification amongst diversity,
Unforced, received gleefully,
Accepted by one and all!

Samskaras - Upbringing with rituals and ceremonies,
Spiritual impressions on conscience,
Starts early in an impressionable age,
Percolates thru' generations as a way of life,
Identified as Indian hood, World over!

Life is guided by spiritualism.
Spiritualism negates negativism,
Faith promotes convictions,
Convictions guide destiny.
Destiny shapes life, ushers prosperity and well-being,
Of the individuals, societies, and the Nation!

Being religious ought to not be restrictive,
Amalgamates diversification,
Religions and regionalism promote diversity,
Diversity amongst communities, societies;
Typical of our Nation,
Makes it unique amongst Nations!

Distortions in history, for self-growth;
Invaders and traitors have been the cause,
Hurting traditions of the natives,
Decimating its history, natives as well;
Vandalized sculptures all over,
Stand silent testimony till date!

Being barbaric, hating its natives,
Mindset of invaders,
Is that the way should have been?
Grow for now, live and let live;
For then you are for the Nation,
Nation is yours, of one and all!

5

Never Give Up

Adjusting to change,
Way to move ahead,
Giving up, is an act of the weak;
Losing without a fight,
Becoming a recluse,
No way, no way!

Making easier for others running through,
It's a wayward reaction to an action,
More difficulties come your way,
Uncaring, withdrawing away;
Life becomes useless anyway,
To become recluse,
No way, no way!

Adjust and change to remain within.
Remain responsible for your own self,
Life is yours, care for it;
Giving up, no way;
It's time to be with you,
Running away is giving up,
No way, no way!

6

Sky

Sky!
A blue roof up above,
Changing colour patterns,
Man, ever engaged to view it,
Inquisitive to know it ever,
Ever busy looking Skywards,
Limitless, an expansive space!

Limitless and vastness;
Deep it is with no limits,
Different shades at different times,
Blue, light blue to white at horizon;
To red, orange, yellow to grey;
All shades depict state of Nature!
No controls in hand!

A roof from within the World,
Off it, expansive, vast, and mysterious!
From calm to rough and tough,
Peeping through the sky,
With intergalactic telescopes,
Now beyond the Universe,
Simply a space holds limitless universe!
Lifeless apparently, may be exuberating with life,
Is still unknown, being explored!

Earth, the only 'Blue Planet' amongst many,
Unexplored ones, similarities obtained;
Millions of light years, distant, far away;
Billions of planets yet to be seen,
Sky creates an aura of roof from Earth,
Is but a space, holding Universe!

Galaxies, Milky way's, Nebulas;
Mysteries unraveled, many still to be;
Recreated in malls, awestruck is one;
Background dark, mysteries abound;
At dark with twinkling stars,
A billion Sun's abound,
With the "Blue Planet" turning grey,
Looking for another close one,
Is it where we would migrate to?

Inquisitive was the mind forever,
Thinking sky-high to reach there,
Moved skywards into the space,
Searching home high above in the sky!
Really! A realm of mind isn't this true;
Still stand on a spinning mass of land!
Apparently straight, obliquely in space!
Even nearly upside down somewhere,
Lucky that we are on the land,
Gravity keeps us stable moving around,
Lest we are thrown skywards!

7
The Saga of Indian Cricket

Brooding over the loss in the T20 World Cup,
Vividly recalled Indian Cricketing Greats,
Time spent reading and seeing them play,
A game quietly followed in the sixties,
More than half a century ago,

Listening commentary with ears glued to the transistors,
Now a cricket crazy country, accepts only winning.
Truly, Indian Cricket was nowhere until fifties;
Still learning to compete in the sixties,
Pataudi became a craze then,
A performer par-excellence,
A bouncer from Griffith, fiery West Indian;
Injured Indian Captain Nari Contractor,
In a tour match in Barbados, then;
Pataudi the New Captain at 21 in 1962,
Expected to revive the sagging fortunes of his team,
A thought, each time he arrived on the crease;
Transistors glued to ears, could he do it again?
Such was his credence.
Honoured in 2013 by BCCI!
"Mansur Ali Khan Pataudi Memorial lecture",
Keeps alive his fabulous contributions!

The spinning quartet spun a web,
Bedi, Chandra, Venky and Prasanna;
The famous four, differing styles;
The best failed to survive,
A combination dreaded by most,
Bedi, a slow left-arm orthodox bowler;
Could bowl at a point, over and again;
Such was his pin point accuracy,
Oft' an opening bowler with shadows lengthening,
Bowling, more overs, towards end of the day,
'Bedi begins from Feroze Shah Kotla Gate end'-
Oft' heard commentary on AIR, expecting change of fortune;
Threatening an early wicket or two!

Chandra, a Right arm-Polio afflicted, leg spinner;
Wisden cricketer of 1972,
Six wickets for 38 at the Oval in 1971,
Got first Test series win for India vs. England,
Prasanna, an off spinner, beat the players in the air;
Became the fastest to get 100 wickets in 20 tests,
An Indian record, now broken by Ashwin;
Venkatraghavan, another off-spinner, 1965 to 83;
Captained two World Cup competitions in 75 and 79,
An elite member of International Umpire Panel for long!
Eknath Solkar, an acclaimed fielder of his times;
As "The diver" stood firmly at forward short-leg,
The "Spinning Quartet" owed much success to him,
See the bowler, batsman play; react a few feet away;
Not an easy task anyway, risking getting hit;
Without helmet then, a suicidal position;
Many a batsmen ill at ease with him in front,
Caught Solkar, kept everyone on the edge.

Flurry of champion players came forth in the 60's,
Sardesai, Wadekar, Vishy, Gavaskar, Engineer-ed success;
Prolific batsmen each one of them,
Sunny, "The little master", stood tall amongst all;
Considered greatest opening batsmen of all time,
2749 runs and 13 centuries versus Windies!
Indian record stands tall till date,
Broke Bradman's Test centuries record of 29,
Seemed unsurpassable then,
Set a new record of 34, stood 19 years;
At 10122, the highest scorer of his times!

Vijay Merchant, Chairman of Selectors,
Called Dilip Sardesai–'Renaissance man of Indian Cricket'!
For a series victory against Windies in 1971,
Later against England,
Brought turnaround in Indian Cricket,
Vanburn Holder and Shillingford to him,
Seemed useless pace bowlers then!
Comparing to Hall and Griffith he faced in 1962,
Gavaskar and Vishy, rookies then, acted as shot in the arm;
Succeeded in bringing confidence amongst team members,
India five down at 75, scored 212 at Kingston Test then!
642 runs, series record, stood for five days;
As Gavaskar went past him!
On the Airport asked to declare, by Customs-
Sardesai quipped,
"I have come here with runs and go back with more".
Scorer of first double century outside India,
One of India's best batsmen against spin attack!

Viswanath's famous square-cut endeared him.
His knocks got many victories to India.
Vengsarkar, stylish batsman, a match winner;
Proved his mettle, batting one down;
With three successive centuries in Tests at Lords,
Even Gavaskar and Sachin failed to hit one there,
By now, Indian cricket had reached prime time!

Then was "Jimmy" exceptionally able Mohinder Amarnath;
Best player facing express pace,
Hero of the finals of World Cup 83,
"Man of the match" in semis and finals,
Most economical wicket-taker when it mattered,
Prodigious son of Lala Amarnath!
Outspoken and a warhorse, "Like father like son";
Dared call selectors, "a bunch of jokers",
"Comeback man of Indian cricket",
Dropped from Indian team, time and again, scaled back in;
Declared out "handling the ball" and "obstructing the field",
Only International player to have been so!

Of the famous cricketer of the yore;
Cricket in India in its early age then,
Lala Amarnath, First Test Captain of Independent India;
His test century on debut, first by an Indian,
Sharp tongued, expert commentator;
To Lala - for expert comments, spoke hard at leisure;
Could bring smile on the face of listeners,
On a dull, insipid days play!

Mankad ran out Bill Brown in second Test,
Versus Australia, series 1947-48;

"Mankading" a legal term to bowl out this way,
Possibly, irritated with unfair advantage -
"Backing up" out of crease, at non-striker's end -
Paused, broke the wicket at non-striker's end before delivering,
First Indian to score 1000 runs and 100 wickets!

Merchant, Hazare, Mankad, Manjrekar;
Unparalleled players of their days,
Cricket with Vijay Merchant-on AIR,
Much sought after program of mid 70's.
Ranjitsinhji, Duleepsinhji, Iftiqar Ali Pataudi,
Players of bygone era!
"Ranji Trophy" and "Duleep Trophy" after famed cricketers,
Played for England before representing India,
C K Nayudu, Mushtaq Ali and Iftiqar Ali Pataudi,
Much playing years lost in World War II!
Kapil then soars the ladder,
Huge World Cup success in "83" waited,
A firm foundation stone had been laid,
A movie '83' released with success,
Revives the story of success,
Broke Hadlee's bowling record of 431 with 434 scalps,
Declared Cricketer of the Century by Wisden in 2002!

In mid 80's, a mad cricket race began in the Middle East;
The deserted pockets began filling,
With muck in 90's, problem of few;
In the news for wrong reasons,
Cricket mafia had started meddling hitherto clean game!
The dust having settled, big time money dug into cricket.

Sehwag, Dravid, Sachin and Saurav;
From North, South, East and West;
Four amongst greatest in World cricket,
Formidable was their combine,
Cricket comes of age, enters period of sublime;
Sachin, "The Master blaster" the highest scorer;
Centurion with Century of Centuries,
The greatest batsman in World cricket,
Brilliance of Saurav, "Tiger of Bengal", the south paw;
Nicknamed "God of off side" by Dravid!
For square cuts and cover drives,
Dravid, "The Wall", made the defense strong;
A treat to watch his copy book batting style!
Not to forget, Kumble, the perfectionist;
Highest wicket-taker for India,
'Perfect-ten' in an inning!
With turn of Century, came a force;
"M S Dhoni", Wicket-Keeper batsman;
"MS" known famously, washed away the dreams of many;
With the competitors left far behind,
No one left in front,
All the Cups from ICC in their cupboard,
Passed the baton to an energetic force!
Virat was his demeanor,
Who flew like a hawk!
Decimated one-by-one, one and all;
Flew higher than could, runs out of energy!

Favourites to win T20 World Cup 2021,
Alas! That was not to be;
History of Indian cricket behind,
Performances well below par,

Thoughtless, a little dysphoric;
Went down in a hurry,
Sank deeper than they could,
A forgotten Cup,
Played in the Middle East,
Bewilderment of 80's in full force again,
Completely off-colour the team this time,
The loss, an abject failure, time to rethink!

Nothing succeeds like success,
Failure guides to weed out problems,
To ride success back again,
Root out favouritism - nepotism and cronyism,
The two enemies at the helm,
Leading the heavy slide seen,
Victories been always limited in true sense!

Is the dream run over?
No, no, not as yet,
With 'Tiger' at the helm,
Recreating the team foremost in mind,
Changes to make dream continues,
History, an on-going process;
"Pataudi Trophy" and "Border-Gavaskar Trophy",
With nine of them in ICC Hall of Fame -
Bedi, Kapil, Sunny, Kumble, Dravid, Sachin, Vinoo Mankad,
Diana Edulji and Sehwag;
The Greatest of Indian Cricketers of all times!
Cricketing greats immortalised with their deeds,
As the saga of Indian cricket continues!

8

Supreme God Shri Krishn

Supreme Godhead, Lotus-eyed;
Krishn, Kanha, Kanhaiya, Govind;
Innumerable names, a reason for all;
Roamed all over,
Established Kingdom in Dwarka,
Eighth Reincarnation of Vishnu!
Revered by Hindus as "Vishnu" Godhead,
Worshipped in His lifetime,
Born on 'Shrawan Krishn Paksh Ashtami',
'Rohini Nakshatra' in the Sky!
At midnight, 5248 years ago!

Under utmost difficult circumstances,
Was born in captivity in Mathura!
Of Tyrant brother of Devaki!
Kans kills all but the Eighth child!
Devaki, Vasudeva's Eighth child was He,
Spontaneous unlocking of doors,
Dead at night, He was outdoors!
Keeps date of killing "Kans-Mama",
As foretold in an "Akashvani"!
"Narayan" born!

The river Yamuna in Spate,
Thus began his journey,
From 'Golok' to 'Gokol',
An exemplary life, He lived;
Under care of foster parents,
Yashoda, Nand Baba of Gokol,
A 'Karmyogi', subject of discussions;
Taught its value to the mortals!

Known and worshipped as 'Radhe',
'Radha-Lakshmi', lifelong association;
The Flutist of the times!
Played 'Raas-Leela' with Gopi's,
Divine dance of love and devotion!
Sneaking Gopi's out of households!
Dead at night in Vrindavan,
As the folklore continues,
Protected natives, lifting "Govardhan Parvat",
Worshipping it instead of "Indra",
Infuriated Indra, King of Heaven, the Rain God;
Torrential rains followed, flood all over;
Recognizes Krishn as Vishnu, bows, withdraws!

Used Sudarshan Chakra,
"Wheel of Carriage", "Wheel of Time"!
Representing auspicious vision,
"The fiercest form of 'Vishnu"!
Held in the rear hand of 'Vishnu',
To kill evil forces of the time,
For establishing Dharma,
His cherished goal,
He killed only four!

Chanoor, Kans, Shishupal, Dantavakra–
The four evil forces of the times!

Peace and 'Prem'-Divine love,
The keywords, close to Krishn,
Prophecies and outcomes, he knew;
Jarasandh, an evil, powerful ruler,
A ruler of Magadh,
Attacked Mathura seventeen times,
Defeated each time by Krishn and Balram,
Krishn Ji had many forays with him,
Reserves slaying Jarasandh for another time,
Taken on by 'Bhim', sometimes later;
In the duel as Jarasandh repeatedly comes alive,
With torn halves reuniting each time!
Krishn signals Bhim to throw the parts across!
As He mitigates the burden of Bhim,
The strongman lay slain!
At the behest of Krishn!
Bhim comes good again!
Riddance from an evil force thus attained!

Continues the evil alliance of,
Jarasandh with Kalayavan,
Another evil King of "Yavanas",
Undefeatable on the battlefield!
A boon granted by Bhagwan Shiv Ji,
Krishn Ji got a formidable city built,
In a far away land, the City of Dwarka!
Becomes "Dwarkadheesh",
The King of the land;
Avoids Kalayavan, saves the natives of Mathura;

As they migrated along,
He knew it all; when, what and how to do!
As He runs away from the battlefield!
Krishn coined "Ranchhod" by Kalayavan,
Chasing Krishn, Kalayavan enters the cave;
Krishn covers Raja Muchkund with "Pitambar",
Sleeping in the cave,
Kalayavan mistook him as Krishn!
Inability to see clearly in low lit cave,
In rage to kill Krishn, gets slained!
As Krishn hides and watches the event,
Kalayavan kicks and wakes up Raja Muchkund!
A mistake that proved too costly,
Fiery rays emanating on seeing him first,
A boon granted by Indra, burns him alive!
Krishn thus saves himself from being seen first!
Cleverly eliminates another evil force of the times,
Away from the battlefield, boon loses its sheen;
The killer is happy and excited to see Krishn!
Follows advice of Krishn-
Performs Tapasya to ward off accumulated sins,
Attains moksha – salvation from rebirth!

Draupadi, Wife of Pandavas,
Sakhi of Krishn tore piece of her Sari-Pallu;
Dresses, bleeding index finger of Krishn,
Hurt, receiving Sudarshan Chakra!
Remembers, returns the favour;
Lengthens robes in "Chirharan Episode",
Hearing her prayers remembering Him,
In the August gathering of Elders, King and Queen;
Infamous episode ordered by Duryodhan,

Carried out by Dushasan,
None helped but Krishn, then in Dwarka;
In a flash reaches out to her in Hastinapur,
Immeasurably lengthens her Sari,
Helps keeping her covered!
Prevents disrobing, a certain humiliation;
Evil designs of Kauravas, thus defeated;
Subserves, three Godly powers-
Omnipresent, Omniscient, Omnipotent!
Worthy of being worshipped as Bhagwan!
An episode, several thousand years later!
Saves the famed, mystic poetess, Mira;
Married to Bhoj Raj, Scion of, "The Rana's of Mewar"!
Protects repeated attempts on her life!
Mira finally leaves the World in 1547!
Merges with Krishn idol, her final abode!

Never shied taking a fight,
Encouraging fighting for 'Rights',
Chief architect of Mahabharata,
Blew 'Panchjanya', declared the war,
Declares start of Kalyug,
For victory of good over evil,
Narrated Gita to Arjun, battle shy;
Shy of picking arms against teachers, brothers!
Before starting the war,
Learns lesson taught by Krishn,
That Soul never dies,
Changes its clothes, renews itself;
Krishn picked up Wheel of Chariot,
Against rampaging, valiant warrior Bhishm,
Showing his immense strength and anger,

Does not use it against him,
Kept his vow, in the epic war!
Would not use arms, prefers being Parthasarthy;
Another name for riding chariot of Parth,
Parth-Arjun, much favoured friend;
War lasting eighteen days in Kurukshetra',
Wiping out the evil forces that existed, then!

Jaydrath, chased by 'Arjun'
With 'Krishn' on the Chariot,
Racing against time,
Arjun's eyes on Sun;
Vows to kill him before the Sunsets!
The task made difficult,
A vow taken in anger, in haste!
Krishn's help does it again!
Sky darkens, as Sudarshan Chakra covers Sun;
Mimicking sunset to mortals!
As 'Chakra-beholder' removes it in time,
Guides Arjun to kill Jaydrath, out in open!
Reminds remorseful Arjun, his goal!
Fulfils his vow, shows the target;
Jaydrath's head, in time;
As the Sun is out there, shining;
Arjun holds his "Gandeev", aims, lets arrow go;
The head that flew,
Falls on his father's lap;
In penance far away!
Killing the evil and its creator, together;
Saves, Arjun from certain death!
Remote hand of Bhagwan Krishn, foreseen;
Abhimanyu's killing thus avenged,

Victory of good over evil, once again!

Attaining the purpose of coming on Earth,
Living fruitful 125 years!
Keeps a date with destiny!
His moving feet that shone like eyes of a deer,
Gets hunted upon by a hunter, Jara!
Apologetic Jara, a rebirth of Bali!
Avenges his killing by Ram,
Reincarnation of Krishn, evil removed then;
Krishn hit by the hunter in hiding,
Jara fulfils wishes of Bali;
An arrow piercing his feet,
Left the World, 3102 BCE!
A Supreme God in his own right,
Worshipped since time immemorial!
An astute statesman, politician;
A friend, remover of evils;
Continues to guide the World till date,
His messages even more relevant today,
On the edge of 'Third World War',
Would it guide the men in time?
Before another tragedy that may rock the World!
Prevent holocaust, his keyword;
Talks to iron out differences - before it is late!

Mahabharat isn't a fiction or a tale!
A final culmination of greed and ego,
End of "Dharma-Yudh" fought to gain 'Rights',
Reasons to fight narrated as "Gita",
Krishn to Arjun shying away from War,
Its narration continues till date!

Of the War that took place in Kurukshetra,
Thirty-six years before He renounced the World,
At 89 fit to destroy the evil, in the epic war;
Possessed all sixteen qualities in one mortal,
Making him Supreme God-head!
The Supreme God-head, "Vishnu Himself",
'Krishn' lives on amongst the mortals!
Worshipped with reverence till date!

9
Beauty lies in the Eyes of Beholder

Beauty is skin deep!
The Philosophers say so;
Righto, as its flesh below;
Unseemly up to the bones,
Covered aesthetically, colored,
Isn't it true, as we see?
Beauty being feminine!

A Beauty in Nature stands in-between!
Complementing each other,
Nature is beauty, femme adds on;
Nature hiding behind,
A femme, in focus, on forefront
Beauty blossoms, at its best.

Love that abounds, twining around;
Beauty in the eyes of beholder!
Something up in the mind; exquisite!
Remains undefined;
Cynosure of all eyes,
Gracefully walks, measured utterance;
A beautiful act, attractive, benumbs;
Mind perceiving ineffable beauty!

It's mind that reads and thinks it all,
Working up at a higher plane,
Exudes true beauty, believes in, within;
Combining beauty and beautiful mind,
Beauty, beautiful mind, rare in one!
Beauty may age, still stays.

Beware of femme fatale!
Feminine wiles with ulterior motives,
Desirous, beauty, uses beauty;
Entrap lovers in deadly traps!
Deserted Mars presented as beautiful!
Lonely, cold and serene;
Beautiful though deadly,
Barren lands, landscapes of all shades;
Nature stays beautiful, all over;
Adage stays, passion takes over,
As Beauty is in the eyes of the beholder!

10

Discordance Dis-synergy All Over

Flow of energy, an action;
Cyclical in nature, a phenomenon in itself;
A physical law follows a pattern;
Refreshes the nature!

Applied safely in nature,
Maintains harmony preserves it;
Nature poised,
Confident, energy synergises!

Disproportional energy, nature estimates;
On the brink of disaster,
Equilibrates, calibrating in unison;
A destabilising force disequilibrates!

Stabiliser upsets the change;
Resetting it, irrevocable its fallout;
Against will of the man, aiming an easy life;
Chief architect, working against the will of the nature!

Energy changes its form,
Cyclical calibration, uniform its norm;
Misguided and dis-synergic,
Disequilibria spread far and wide!

Energy released changes the norm,
Self-propagation, motive ulterior;
Outcome, so disturbing;
Hurdles created, as nature keeps changing.

Free for all, concept of effortless gain;
The gain, nevertheless, is at a price!
Takes away freedom of mind,
Man gets enslaved, disequilibrium prevail.

Mind only a follower, gains only slight;
Freebies serves, creates a bond so tight;
Enslaved, a subservient, for good;
Forces controlling such change, only gains!

The incorrigible, gains without a fight;
Mind unlearns, forget travails to survive;
Freebies for survival, fails to thrive;
Withdrawn, economic crisis, its fallout!

Herald's unsocial movement,
Manipulator motivated to prevail;
Changes get so perverse, as nothing is for free;
Societies, Nations get bonded, unserved!

The concept begins to interfere, hurts;
The corrupts, the unsocial, takes a big leap;
Accepting gains for free stands rejected;
Law of nature, disturbed for all times!

Natives of the land, affected, rejected;
Displaced by the high and mighty,
Annihilation grows, new order prevails;
For a while, is physics, of the societal loss!

Application of science is all over,
As the student of science takes over the reins;
Manipulates energy for self-propagation,
Dis-synergises, spreads discordance all over!

Grabbing power, an area gets corrupted;
The problem that emanates,
Spreads its wings in the region,
Slowly right across the Nation!

Invasion of social evils laid, infirmly so;
Destabilising known practices,
Wins percentage, prospers, and propagates;
Weakens the society as it disintegrates!

Evil practices, across the nation, soars;
Disintegration begins; discordance spreads its wings,
Cultural, social clumsiness sweeps thru'!
Nip the evil in time, live with challenges, survive.

It's realisation in time,
Identify, defeat evil designs, outright;
Strengthen moral values, stabilises, and braces the Nation!
Dis-synergy, discordant energies, mustn't let stay!

11

Surveillance Needless

Is it a free world we live in?
Under constant glare and surveillance,
One and all, all aspects of life;
Every aspect of privacy under the scanner,
Infringes basic rights of individuals,
Right from the skies, cameras in space;
Keeps a watch on aspects hitherto uncovered!
It's surveillance all the time!

Since man gained control of space,
Denying rivals freedom of action from space,
Spy satellites to keep a tab over the rivals,
Hegemony over the rest, his sole aim;
Wars and battles won, strength not enough;
Winning based on actions with knowledge prior,
Critical positions thru' images,
World, restive and competitive;
Terrain watch, gazing boundaries across;
Not only their own but beyond,
Scanning stars, galaxies, and even far away!

Technologies to find life existing elsewhere,
Migrating sole aim as resources exhaust on Earth,
No sense of responsibility, no care taken;
Abandon after using, a problem getting acute;

Here there and everywhere,
Problems remain the same,
Checks to master all, keep controls in hand;
Checking the Nature, safety checks incomplete;
It's surveillance all the time!

Games played for entertainment,
Now gazed thru' remote eye,
Professionals, play for livelihood;
Sole breadwinners kept on tenterhooks,
Playing for masters, fat some salaries they play for;
Remain silent, knowing weakness recorded;
On display, howsoever unprofessional it be,
For money is "All that Matters"!
For surveillance is there all the way!

Despite human eyes and mind involved,
Umpiring decisions ultimate, Oh! No longer!
On the ground not enough, third umpire matters;
Technical supports, technicalities involved;
Hawkeye to declare a person off the game,
Is it in the spirit of the game, is it worth?
Playing to entertain, irrelevant now;
It's surveillance time, all the time!

"Winning or losing not important", an adage;
Spirit of game no longer a part,
Aiming to win, strategies changed;
Technical aspects checked, affect competitions?
Games played to galleries, betting with insiders;
Survive in game, excelling for long, not easy now;
Top-notch players withering away!

Misuse of surveillance all the way!

In-camera recordings, shared and publicised;
Weaknesses caught, human eyes not trained to;
Ability to check core weakness of the best,
Confirmed time and again, coaching with laptops;
Advisory to players from information therein,
Now much in use in cricket,
Happened in Edgbaston, a bouncer signaled;
Coach knew weakness; the player got caught out;
Surveillance this time used for winning ways!

Is this any gamesmanship?
Sportsman spirit at stake,
Oh! No worries, not important anymore;
Manipulators outside now control the game,
Making more than players in the game!
Developing sports or destroying its spirit!
Watergate scandal should have been normal then,
Winning only motive, is same anyway;
Computer-guided is playing beyond one's ability,
Advantage surveillance used for winning ways!

Playing as guided by advisers a common sighting,
Deciding victor and loser, ability ignored;
To win on one's ability, under question;
Integrity of the spirit of the game in doubt,
Impression created, of loss of interest;
Time to keep internal cameras on,
Mitigate surveillance, need of the hour;
Matches of yesteryears, interesting to watch;
Performances, their own, the way they played;

Results unanticipated, kept one interested till the end,
Surveillance used; unfair advantage taken!

Result predicted before with graphical swings,
Kills the interest, why even see, if result known;
See the percent swing, decide if worth watching;
Seeing is to confirm, if the game followed the pattern;
Betting and match-fixing a recent scourge,
Mathematical predictions getting truer now,
Ability to predict victor out of multiple teams!
In a way, match-fixing or mathematical issues!
With no interest left, let declare winner too!
Winner's trophy before the tournament,
Would kill the excitement the game played for!
Surveillance, manipulates interest left in the game!

Indian hockey, eight times Olympic champions;
Wizardry of legendary Dhyan Chand examined,
Use of the hockey stick given a close look!
With time rules changed the way the game played!
Yesteryear's winners been pushed out of race,
Rules manipulated, turf changed, Astroturf now;
Artificial turf used to trample the champions,
Out manipulated with rules changed,
Champions left high and dry, for years;
Played under flood lights, four directions;
Four shadows, warns a player around;
Surveillance used to manipulate,
Rules manipulated, checking winning ways!
Now limping back to glory days back again!

With weaknesses exposed, rivals gain;
Unknown previously gets known;
Made to play unplayable, the winner ends a loser,
How useless things could get!
Concept that has changed the game,
Financial interests prevents winning over and again,
Abiding with times, forget rights;
Learn to live and thrive!
Compete to win, whatever that takes one to!
Surveillance has changed the games now played!
Needless surveillance demotivates all!

12

Free is Dangerous

Bonded in chains,
Seems dangerous to be,
Lambasted by the Right's group,
Absolute free is ridiculous, dangerous to be.

Born free, is for few to be;
Normal in the animal World,
Noble that they are,
Not dangerous beyond they live!

Though free is good to be,
In limits, is what humans need be?
Free to do unwanted and undesirable,
Could out-manipulate one and the support!

Yeah, too sick to always be free;
It is living dangerously,
Dangers lurks from all quarters,
Chaotic gets the life!

Societies and Nations,
Who care not, the way they live;
Eat every conceivable item,
Spread dangers all over.

Perilously close on, our northern neighbour;
Nonchalant is the way they live,
Cause of diseases, frequently for decades;
Creators of pandemics all over!

We pray that they learn to live,
Care for the way they live,
The actions go along as they think;
Actions that affecting others, isn't worthy enough!

Creators of Bird flu, now Neo-Corona;
Miseries and concern, around the Globe;
The World on alert,
Deaths and scare in 2020 as never before!

Created a monster, bio-warfare it's been;
An invisible enemy of mankind,
Let it spread, through land and air;
Modes of travel now fast, faster it spread.

Conveniently helped spreading,
Till it went around the globe,
To distant lands, across the oceans;
Silent were they till the fingers pointed!

Satisfied to spread the pandemic,
Millions affected as deaths rolled over,
Experiments in Wuhan laboratory,
Financed and supported caused upheavals!

Years of financial supports to the unknown,
Been the cause, a worrisome one;

Till 1972 living in the World of their own,
"Ping-Pong Policy" got them to the fore!

Students studied, gained experience;
Educated in the top Universities of West,
Brought technologies to their land,
Groomed, educated, and economically strengthened!

A challenge to those, got support from;
Uncaring as they lived their lives,
Experimented the way they thought was right,
Paying penalties as they get challenged!

Powerful now, hegemonic tendencies obvious;
Living dangerously with neighbours,
At war they have always been,
For might is right, as the phrase goes!

Was it right then in 1972?
Awakened a sleeping giant,
With the energies transferred now,
Hiring cheap labor helped capturing markets all over!

A cause of strife, competition adverse;
Powers now transferred,
Poor were the notions, results adverse;
Close to self-destruction, self inflicted it's been.

Some sort of chains, so important it is;
Binds one to a pattern,
Controls unchecked, freedom total;
Dangerous it is, all have seen.

Pearl Harbor bombing to Ping-Pong Policy,
Sleeping giants awakened,
Stirred and shook the World,
Cost of cheap labor, this time it's been!

One thing is clear now,
Help to grow an ignoble civilization,
Self destruction, over a period;
Is all it has served!

Now standing tall amongst Nations,
Full of energy and strength,
Power-hungry that they are,
Annihilation of nations, all that they do!

Outwitting a nation like this,
Collective responsibility,
Isolation economic, social and intellectual;
A way that is left to do!

13
The Nature Within

Height of anger,
That began to boil,
That formed the fumes,
That kept going up,
Till go no more!
Lost its heat,
Formed the Clouds,
Collected high up,
Shows its power,
Began to roll!
Thunderbolt,
Lightening in Sky,
Huff and puff!
Flies with the wind,
To distant lands –
From sea to mountains –
Passes over the land,
With all its might!
Thunderbolt,
Blew its fuse,
Lightening in Sky!
Black and White!
Now off-steam!
Begins to cool,
Got so heavy,

Lost its power,
Grip got lose,
Can hold no more,
Changes its form!
Now, helpless and crying!
Water rolls down,
Showers so sharp,
Comes down fast!
All over the land,
With lots of streams,
Rivers now flowing,
Clouds up there,
Now seem nowhere,
Cloudless Skies,
From Black to Blue,
Life on a roll!
Parched lands got wet,
All that's up,
Always comes down,
Distributes it even,
Call it Nature's balancing act!

Was this all within!
Up in the mind,
Attributed to Nature!
Red eyes, furious in anger;
The flow, cleanses it all;
Fluttering no more!
Life on a roll!
Reflects, the Nature within!

14

Through

I kept watching,
Imagining silently,
Within,
The life nearly through,
All the guys who knew,
The immense support,
With me,
For me,
Closes with me,
Watching the stars,
At night, twinkling;
Till they fade away!

15

Struggle, a Phase of Life

When things go wrong,
Mind out of control,
Take courage from happenings,
Beyond you, far away!

When circumstances are out of control,
For anyone, anywhere;
Keeps mind and soul in unison,
Twosome shall work it out, never fails!

For soul is the master controller,
Of belief, effort and emotion,
Mind of acumen, intellect and knowledge,
Twosome together finds solutions!

On the horizon, solutions are many;
Listen to the alter ego, the sixth sense,
Truth hidden within, transforms you;
Newer phase begins thereon!

16

Betrayals Betraying Our Own

Vulnerable since 1001 CE,
Mistook aliens to our land, their own,
Our own, secluded by our own;
Invited outsiders, as our own;
Got finished off, killing our own!

Failing to identify our own,
Divulging weaknesses, our own;
To outsiders, not our own;
Traitors born amongst our own,
To wrest control from our own!

Working against our own,
Soon got cornered and cordoned,
Handed over our own,
To warlords from far-off lands,
Giving new dimensions to problems,
Essentially our own!

Invaders tortured and ruled our own!
Invited to fight, a bitter truth, with our own;
Lust for things on land, stayed forevermore;
Without much fighting, took over, ruled ruthlessly.
Lived for ages, as if it was their own!

Divided in regions, Kingdoms were many;
All fighting for one-upmanship, in the land, our own!
Forgot outsiders were not their own!
Conniving with others defeated their own!

Failed Prithviraj, Maharana's, and Maratha's!
Handed over our own, fighting for land not their own;
Ruled by the Mughals, invaders from the West-
The Britishers then did the rest!

Freedom struggle, hands joined,
Got it after much chaos!
Forced out or left, debated, not important;
Motherland divided; two Nations were born!
Thus, came out India with new dreams!

Out of the clutches of invaders, for far too long;
Aftermath issues, its handling important;
Many of those who ruled and controlled,
Joined hands, continued to divide, to politically survive!
Problems of undivided land still continues,
Further divided the Nation betrayed our own!

Thus, living with a facade created;
By the wily and the crafty!
Periodic spells of darkness, thrusted upon;
Once again, betraying our own;
Living with false promises,
Poor vision continues, as ever before!

Similar happenings, World over!
The rulers, who ruled, came from all over;
Crushed the inhabitants, oppressed them;
Plundered, looted and returned!

Rioting, arson still continues,
History been created, left this on us, mate;
We say proudly though-
We live in the only Nation, a mix-up of religions;
Recognise aliens to the land, as our own!

Hoping that the turmoil in mind gets soon over,
Betraying our own, traitors born again;
Loyalty is fidelity with our own,
Nation needs your time, forget playing with our own.

An autoimmune reaction of some sort,
Auto-rejection, self-destructive; struggle continues;
Living and managing well, despite mix-up of all;
We are one of the many "Secular Nations" known!
Secularism is very strong, in our own!

17

Truths as Myths

With the passage of time,
History lost and refreshed,
With invaders taking over the land,
Destroyed, manipulated, and ruled ruthlessly;
For nearly a thousand years!

Plundered and attempts to alter the culture!
Yet, survived and continued to thrive!
Hindus, once the only ones to be on the land,
Many more added up with time,
Invaders ended converting many more!

Political needs continued to divide,
Masses used on secular pretext,
The only Secular State in the World with equal rights!
Constitutional change brought it in 1976!
A civilization to be the oldest and once developed!

The majority continues to suffer,
Glorious has been its spiritual growth,
Religious descriptions, authored;
Have been legendary figures!
A great experience these have been
Gave directions the way to live!

But many still believe if it ever were,
A creation of mind even if it were,
A realm of mind creates falsehood.
It's time to let the truth prevail,
Fact-finding for their existence,
Reasons to believe it to be true;
A message for all, guidance after all!

We believe all of these were true!
For science believe in evidence,
Many evidences have come rolling by,
All believe in except for a few,
For they all existed and it's true,
Its glorious past as mythology!
Neither was our belief nor is it true!

All to destroy its culture not their own,
'Mythos' itself a Greek Word,
Described their Mythos, their cultural legends!
A figment of imagination!
Who enforced 'Mythos' to our legends?
Raises doubts on the history of our land!

Impressions created by invaders,
To call it as falsehood and untrue,
Now even the dates have been confirmed!
Narrations and relations so perfect,
Places existed were all real!

"Ram" and "Ramayan",
"Krishn" and "Mahabharat",
"Gita" and "Krishn",
From "Ayodhya" to "Dwarka",
"Sita" to "Radha",
"Kashi" to "Mathura",
A part of our glorious past,
It's glorious present!
Gave messages true till date,
To be proud of and believed!
Narratives and details, so true;
Serials produced over years,
Have become famous and seen,
Appreciated and understood!

The very basis of an ancient civilization,
Still famous as "Bharat", A Great Nation!
Surrounded by Oceans on three sides,
Bay of Bengal in South-East,
Arabian Sea in South-West; and
Only Ocean known after a Nation since 1515 CE,
"As Hind Mahasagar"- Indian Ocean in South!
In Latin as "Oceanus Orientalis Indicus" before!
A Nation located in the centre, it's head!

18

Wars to Dominate

Aśoka's sense of propriety,
Had Law of Piety,
Kalinga war proved his nemesis,
Immense loss of lives for petty reason!

Took Buddhism,
Children helped it spread,
Now opposite is seen,
War crimes continue.

Citizens blocking adversaries,
Brave are they, sufferings utmost;
Affronted with tanks,
They care not for they value to be free.

Freedom must be respected,
Rules guarded by the United Nations,
Understanding still very flimsy,
Muscles are flexed by the strong to rule.

It's seen day after day!
As the nations get drawn in the war,
Flimsy reasons, more often;
To dominate, only reason!

Winning it,
Is all important,
Freedom of no value to a few,
No rules, to spread the rule.

In the war that broke a year ago,
There is complete breakdown of rules,
For "Everything is fair in love and war",
Is but true!

19
Nepotism Cronyism a Disgrace

Nepotism and Cronyism,
Disgraceful favouritism!
Needy and worthy left out,
Aspirations, crushed, no space to grow!

Nepotism is promoting kinship;
Cronyism stands for friends,
Starts for personal gains,
Evil practices, affect common man;
No Godfather of their own!

Widespread in politics, politicians;
Corrupts with finances in control,
Gains extreme power with meteoric rise,
Enjoying working with cronies,
In key positions, irrespective of qualifications;
Able disabled, out of reckoning!

The space for growth restricted,
Only for a few selected to be,
See antagonism at work,
Working for and controlled by cronies,
Ugly face of nepotism, cronyism, at play!

The worthy and brilliant,
Under no consideration!
Close to powers, way to stay and thrive!
Disenchantment at work,
Cronyism, Nepotism at play!

Dynastic rule in pluralism,
Instances of nepotism, cronyism!
How hard one may try, harder to displace;
Ability and able be the trusted colleague,
The criteria in a happening society!

Condemned in Epics!
Nepotism, cronyism in Indian politics,
As a matter of fact, is all over;
Undeserved, crooked, survive, and thrive!
Partiality in awarding jobs, a pattern!

Criteria for opportunity survive and perform;
Condemned, by Thiruvalluvar;
Indian philosopher of 1st BCE,
Called nepotism, "Evil and unwise"!
Love and liking to select an unfit for the job;
Endless follies follow, affecting the selector!

Nepotism and cronyism,
Evil practices as they are,
Provide stability, continuity to a selected few!
Uproot it with all your might,
The deserving gets ignored, no more!

Reservations for selections,
A crude form of favouritism,
Created for political gains,
Able, meritorious rejected over favoured,
Have no place in societies,
Promotional time gone much beyond!

Favouritism is the key,
From home, school to workplace;
Cut throat competition, amongst professionals;
Disillusionment at work,
Cronyism, nepotism on display!

Does its tricks, in the sports arena too;
Nepotism in business, in the Churches,
In the high places in the land!
Must it be there if selection is fair?
Abilities recognized a way to go ahead!

Dislodging one in favour of the other,
Out of reckoning over the least able,
For the talented be rightfully judged,
Gains rightful position and adjudged,
If nepotism, cronyism be silenced forever!

See none being robbed again,
Sporadic public uprising be seen,
To be uniformly seen against.
Be the norm in societies!
Denounce it vigorously, effectively!

Succumbing, losing life, for failing;
An avoidable loss must sink in one and all,
Life is precious, for no one to lose it;
To nepotism, cronyism, nowhere again!

20
Perils on, Nature at War

World, once in a state of molten lava,
Began development of Nature,
Shaped up in billions of years,
As the land began to cool, made to live;
Water and air, a miracle it added;
Favoured the life to be, safe to exist;
The Nature intends to go along,
As the life flows and blends with it!
Glory seen, is the glory of Nature been!

Sadly, it has taken a nose-dive,
Science for comfort, been the cause;
Promised but, failed, safety its concerns,
Nature impacted with mind convoluted,
With Industrialisation, it began;
The Climate that sustained plunges now,
Twisting the temperatures all over,
1°C rise in temperature it's been, since!

Scientific discoveries followed soon,
Internal combustion engines in fray,
The products meant for comfort,
Followed briskly, easing lifestyles;
Speeding up the life, now in fast gear!
Subtle change began to disturb it;

Now polluted, altered with discoveries;
Climate altered added miseries!
Things began worsening fast,
Scientists worried now, been left aghast!
Changes that happened in million years,
Began happening in a lifetime!

Joe, Brian, and Jonathan in Eighties,
Discovered and described the hole,
Ozone hole, over Atlantic, been big!
Ozone layer, a shield it's been;
Protecting the Nature, all it did;
Dread its loss, effect so profuse;
Ultra-violet rays from the Sun!
How dangerous to life it's been!
Radiations now through the hole,
Its man pitied against man, now left to contain!

Ozone hole in stratosphere, the outer layer;
Increased in size, in the spring time;
Release of gases, bromine, and chlorine;
Compounds of carbon been the cause,
Activity of man, its reason;
White with snow and ice for long,
Changes on Poles, discernible now;
Life survived for long, despite the rough,
Now began melting with the rising seas,
The release of carbon acidifies the seas,
Marine life getting downsized,
Species vanishing fast!
The Green-house gases,
That entraps the heat, radiates all over;

That warmed the Earth, that began to cheat;
That added the gloom, snow began melting fast;
Polar bears, penguins, and seals, lives endangered;
Atmosphere that survived and saved the life;
Began to crumble, all too fast!

No time left to think now!
Foot faulted with discoveries, pitfalls many,
Planners working thoughtlessly,
Nature did the rest, responded ceaselessly!
The Nature that brought life on Earth!
Life is in a 'State of Peril' on Earth!
Need to act responsibly now,
Shredding comfort, not an iota;
Artificial world man now lives in,
Uncomprehending dangers ahead!
Impairment of nature now intense!
Thunderstorms, hurricanes all so common;
Floods in rivers all over the globe,
Asymmetric progression of monsoon!
Himalayas with unnatural lakes,
Moisture with heat, been the cause!

Inconsistent rainfall on the land,
A deluge here, scarce there;
The rivers persistently on the rise,
Floods, hurricanes intense all over,
Recurring all around the world,
Many coastal cities set to submerge,
With rising and advancing seas!
Rising by a meter, by the turn of century;
River's flow into sea now in jeopardy,

Back flow of seas, rising river;
Water flows, Intense floods all over!
Sums up, the change so subtle it's been;
Marooning cities, how horrible could it be!
Many coastal cities set to submerge!

Movement with life stock enmasse,
Fighting for every inch of land,
Diseases and pandemics to be on rise,
With millions of people likely to perish!
As the scenario turns difficult for man,
It's prudent to know it now!
Of man-made mistakes, issues are many;
Reverse the issues, imminent, trending now,
The process that began for comfort,
It's time to abandon, one and all;
Else wait, until nature enforces, gets tough!

Nature is resetting the cause,
Cares little for the survival of man,
Survival of man now getting difficult,
Modest living now, expected to be;
Be the norm, acceptable to all;
Life drifting to Stone-age for survival,
Be spontaneous or be enforced upon!
See the change, live and let live or let it adrift,
Doomsday for then will not be far away!
Apply brakes, little time left;
Sustain the Nature, important than ever;
Live to save life of all, else die for destroying it!

Can the philosophers and planners unite?
Never so important it's been,
Forget financial gains,
Else let problems arise, go down along with it;
Consistency in inconsistencies,
Probability of the improbable,
Abnormal natural phenomenon on rise,
Extinction of life on Earth now nears,
Considered improbable till now,
Is now insight!
In the Himalayas, Europe, and in New York now,
Loss of life as never before!
Disasters uncommon, now routine;
Stark happenings all over,
Clearly labeled, 'Due to nature change'!

Time to get the act together,
As World Powers sit and decide,
Montreal Protocol, Helsinki Meet to Paris Climate Agreement;
Things agreed upon, slow its progress;
Ecological foot prints versus global ecological footprints,
Its local pressures against global ones,
Avoid 2°C rise of global temperature by end of century,
New norm, diligently to pursue upon;
Signatories agree to reduce carbon emissions,
Not all countries have joined and signed!
Agree to disagree, not the way to be!

Time to act now, right now;
Make it a people's movement,
By the people, for the people;
Precipitating reasons to wind-up now,
Authorities have failed all over!
Aided with living for comfortable life,
It's not their cause, not the only to suffer;
Save the nature now adrift, life at risk;
Wage war against nature's destruction,
Love to live and thrive!
Pray, warnings not are ignored, for sure!
Perils ahead, Nature at war!
Turn the table to support the nature,
Do it, do it now, just right now!

21

Nature's Devastation

Held together with mud and lava,
Rose up the Himalayas,
On Continental shift,
Forty to fifty million years ago!

Washed since, weathered the storm;
Man-made excesses, smashes it up;
In a punitive mood, Nature is;
Cloud bursts now often, rising ever before!

Frequent deluge, washed its glue;
That held the rocks for all so long,
Unstuck; rocks and stones, free to roll,
It's raining rocks and stones, on a free roll!

Problems now common, seen World over;
Landslides in Kinnaur and Noney,
Towns in Himachal Pradesh and Manipur,
Loss of lives huge, ungainly activity of man;
Shows up, time and again!

It's 'Celestial Dance', call 'Tandav Nritya',
A Cosmic-dance, not far away, how havoc could it be?
The Creator and the destroyer zeroing in,

Punishes man, wrecking it! Man stands exposed!
Would it be his shortest stay!
The most intelligent amongst beings!
Ends up punishing one and all!

The mistakes done over years, giving telling blows;
Sewing it together, only act now to do;
Salvable as of now, nature needs your time!
Warning signs, known for long, lousy ways;
Overlooking all along, fighting for reasons,
Is it binge-watching, wasting time;
For he knows it's out of hand?

Down with hurricanes, floods, cold front, drought in US,
Drought and famines in horn of Africa,
Wild fires in US, Siberia and Australia,
Rising temperatures, that melts the glaciers;
Polar ice caps, snow wherever it be,
Rising sea levels, drowning cities away;
Predictably in not many years as of now!

Venezuela first country to be bereft of glaciers!
The Sixth glacier melts, ten years in advance!
US Environment Protection Agencies on Clean Air Act,
Jolted with Apex Court's Order that day!
Favouring coal companies, carbon emissions uncontrolled;
Economical attention, promoting pollution, fated to be;
Financial gains and comforts, all that matters!
World on mercy of the strong and mighty!
Shouldn't be, shouldn't be;
Time for all to unite, suppressing, not to be!

It's Nature's devastation, effectuating now;
Of no consequence, finances would be;
Formal bankruptcy, stocks going to zero;
Its nature change, forcing efforts to a nought;
Unpleasant challenges, rocking the world;
Time to check one by one, be safe, live safely;
Nature cares a damn, clueless?
No time to be! Indiscrimination, challenging the Nature;
Living with comforts, costly it would be!
We have devastated the nature as far as it could be!

22

Nature Change now Constant

In this World, change is constant;
It's law of the nature!
Constant change turning against life,
Much too early, to activities of the man;
Willfully going against the nature!
Started biting, hitting man and life all around!

Primarily, a lifestyle problem;
It's the change,
That may be obstreperous,
That need be contained,
That's changing the ecology,
Pollution, a new constant change now all over!

Scrutinise the change,
Nature nearly constant stood the test of time,
For long, acceptable, and viable;
Could it get so wild, willful curse?
The power wielding effects of man!
Influenced change, now no more constant!

Changing the course of river!
Action so adverse, calamitous;
Through obstructions, overflows;
Landslides, to cloud bursts;

Upsetting the ecology,
Destroying lives, a constant change, it's been!

An attempt to change Beas River's course,
Failed for good, checked in time;
Prevented a certain holocaust!
Future of man stays in jeopardy, out of control;
Innumerable mistakes continue unchecked;
It's Man versus Man!
An eternal conflict for dominance!

Check ongoing wars with nature is at war!
Destruction and survival interlocked,
Besieged with issues,
Fighting with his mind,
Time to listen to mentor,
An urgent need to respond, in time;
Delay now against own survival! No longer in hand!

Nature, dynamic, takes its call;
As man forges with concepts entangled,
Nature misfires as man struggles;
Acts the only way it knows, works;
Follows its free will,
Live and let die! The formula it envisages!

In a flash, nature can flatten the life on Earth!
Its brute force can reset those blameworthy!
Fate nearly sealed with follies, the nature is pushing its free
will, No distinctions it makes!
Time to learn to live and survive!
Live and let live! To thrive!

Intelligence to upstage it one last time,
Five mass extinctions been, sixth one on,
Nature brought him to life, the fifth time;
Grave danger to life with sixth one on,
Confused, living with constant change;
Living on precariously, knows not of morrow!

Disruptive technologies use no more;
It's time to realise mistakes,
Uproot them to survive, one last time;
Attempting to save the nature!
Stop climate change;
Earnestly pray for him to succeed!
Survival utmost in mind, for change is constant!
Now largely out of control!
Climate is constantly changing, disturbing;
Time to act before it gets too late!

23

Climate Change Deterrence

Jack went up...and Jill came rolling after,
But for a pail of water!
An old nursery rhyme!
Now water went up to form those clouds;
Torrential downpour,
With surging streams,
That washed the hill,
That washed the glue,
That held the rocks,
With Jacks and Jills,
Gone up the hill, and
Stones came rolling after!

Care for now!
Dear, Jacks and Jills!
Don't go to the hill,
During heavy downpour!
For many went up!
And lost their lives,
As "Breaking News"!
Mourns the loss!
Of the precious lives!
When stones came rolling on them!
Cos of climate change,
In changing times,

Sew it right,
Sew in time!
Change it now,
Change it right;
Time to do it,
Do it, do it, do it, now!
Do it, do it, do it, right now!

24

Manipulating History

History details are written facts,
Ancient manuscripts on "Bhoj Patra"-
A peel of bark of tree in Himalayas,
Used as paper to write and record,
Documented in local vernacular of the times,
Multilingual translations spread much later;
Right across the World!
Facts posted for posterity!

Verbal transcending information's thru generations,
Most difficult to change, facts surface;
By and large facts are true,
Not always is also true,
Vitiates associations,
History written as truth, avoids myths;
Truths floated as myths, lowers its value;
Manipulators change history,
Spread canard to suit their purpose!
Hiding behind the canard, the untruth thrives!

How wrong could it get!
Manipulate untrue as truth of the past,
Respect disregarded; motives ulterior;
Why should they do?
Alter the facts, change the truth;

Fictitious information, changes history;
Impact minds, falsehood propagates;
Until memory loses over a period,
Reflecting what is not, made to believe;
By the powerful, the sly of the times;
For people to follow a pattern,
Base the way of lives, on dotted lines;
Thoughts affected; facts re-created!
For the text have changed, sayings left;
Truth now turns into myths, how untrue!
True history now untrue stories,
It's time to upstage the untruth!

Nature's history, its own, hard facts;
Lay buried in the layers of earth, its own;
Permanent in nature, explored, noted;
In the air, transient change, changes its contents;
Transient then, now permanent,
As part of changing nature,
Changes in nature is recorded history,
Natural or artifact, to human activities;
To artificial mode of living of man,
Protecting self from harsh nature!

Historical facts of the times, gone by;
Lay buried in the layers of Earth!
To battles, wars, natural calamities;
Different eras on the earth recorded,
Paleontology, fossilised facts of life on Earth;
A part of archaeological survey!

Earthquakes, volcanoes, asteroid impact and fires;
Changed the history of Earth, life on Earth!
Distorted history, impacts sooner or later;
Known facts ignored, get pronounced with times!

Disappearance of the generations,
Analysed later, albeit alterations and distortions;
Full-fledged War, disputed!
Modus operandi to distort the facts!
Mighty gets it revised, as might is right;
Analysis later, of a civilisation wiped off;
Confirms it otherwise!
Just a dispute, spreading what's untrue;
History in making, reasons known, and truth lies buried;
The vicious facts tell if it was a dispute or an act of war!
Wiping off to getting wiped out,
Temporary erasure, now permanent!

Manipulating history considered crime!
Punishable with imprisonment!
Distortion of historical records!
Introduced negations, denialism,
Falsify-distort historical records,
Burning of books, slaughtering texts of scholars;
Burnt Nalanda University stands as testimony,
Manipulating history as if it never was!
Preserving history, facts need revisiting!
Undoing wrong-doings of the past,
A monumental duty, upholding it, a national pride!
Imbibing history, an important possession;
Countrymen with no insight of past!
Future remains shaky, under stress;

Fail to react, as they must, prevent uninvited change!
Manipulations galore, to be challenged,
Await revisions – corrections!
Only pro do corrections!

25

Careless No Concern

Care not what you lived for!
Care not, damned one and all!
Worried, you lived to care for your own,
Cared for your family, nation;
Groups of nations, hegemonistic allies exist;
Set to conquer, destroy, and rule, weaker nations;
Create fear with nuclear arsenals!
Bothered you to fight to exist!
Gained selling arms of mass destruction,
Could use them all, careless with no concern!

Newer technologies, worked upon;
Hypersonic weapons now developed,
Now testing the untested!
Hegemonic tendencies, newer grounds to test on;
Ending the adversaries quickly,
Careless, no concern at all!

But do worry of enablers, who cared;
The plants, the animals, the unknown, terrestrial, aquatic;
On a backdrop of uneven terrains,
A beautiful Nature that developed,
Gave amenities, to enjoy, prospering;
Were preyed upon, devoured, to thrive;
Invalids were they, physically, mentally;

Know not the motives fighting for;
Explain them the outcome!
Establishing egoistically, thou' prevails;
On the threshold of destruction, biting the dust!
Could've lived endlessly on, if not for you;
Careless, no remorse, not concerned at all!

Destroyed the nature that protected the man,
That made you thrive, used up to its core;
Destruction of man seems near now,
The man that survived two World Wars,
With the third on horizon!
Destruction could reach its zenith!
Drawing end of the World, of one and all!

Most violent amongst the living!
Still only second to the Nature!
Wait until the day it turns the tables!
Releases energy enormous!
Unleashing its own nuclear button,
Dispossess you of your own!
In a flash can destroy your concepts,
Clueless now to contain its might!
Man is out to destroy destiny of all!

Leaves in the end "A lifeless Planet,"
The nature left, reads blue print of past!
Tells the tales to the subsequent,
Archaeological evidence if someone could survey,
Gives a damn to the man who damned it all!
For you were careless, no remorse, not concerned at all!

26

Economic Power and Wars

Ego, Money, Power, the three evil forces;
Greed follows, to have even more,
Rightfully or unjustly though,
Weapons to corner adversaries;
Bickering starts off, follows the war!

Adverse effects known,
The results so perverse,
Civilisations been destroyed,
Equipped, fights for power absolute;
No barriers, invaders cross them all.

Borders breached; war is on;
Went even across the oceans,
Mayan civilisation destroyed, no way;
Identities of invaders got erased,
Surviving in new lands, no praise!

"Gita" narration by Shri Krishn,
Mahabharat, a dreaded war that followed;
An abject lesson to all,
Time becomes the healer,
The invaders ridiculed by the generations!

Failing to avert, greed been the cause;
Finishing off the greedy, attain all;
Two kinships fighting for Kingdom,
One wanting to usurp, other opposes;
Give the least, reject, fight to lose!

Lay slain at the end of the epic battle,
An eighteen days battle!
The battlefield, Kurukshetra;
Thousands lay dead, none gained;
Mahabharat, a needless war, lesson to all!

Lesson to humanity all over!
Widely read, true, still selects war;
Unholy mix-up of ego, money, and power;
Results consistently bad,
Finishes it all, bereft of all!

Till the three of these combines,
A war is the net result!
The war that erupts, whenever, wherever;
Bad mix-up of the three,
Destroys the destinies of one and all,
Lessons from "Gita", tells it all!

27

It's Yesterday Once More

Remember the dates,
July 1945 the month,
Sixth year of World War raging,
Two Olympics abandoned,
India missed two golds in hockey,
Bradman a few centuries,
Germany surrendered, out of reckoning then;
Japan unconquered till then!

Power unleashed, controlling the uncontrollable;
World destiny changed forever,
World War II was nearly at its end,
Pearl harbour bombing by Japan,
A venture to get combatant on negotiating table,
Destined to go awry, as history unfold;
Awaken a sleeping giant,
Allies Manhattan project completed!

Month, July 1945,
Two atom bombs prepared,
Uranium type, Little-boy;
Gun-type, fission weapon it was;
The other, Plutonium type, Fat-man;
Implosion type was that;
Potsdam declaration, 26th July-the date;

Unconditional surrender of Japanese forces, its aim!

No-one knew the havoc that could be,
UK consented, US took the ordeal;
B-29 Bombers used to use the hitherto unused,
Little-boy dropped on the eleventh day,
6th August 1945, the day the humanity lay low;
Hiroshima stood ruined, war continued,
Third day from that day, 9th August 1945;
Fat-man did the rest; unfortunate city, Nagasaki!

City devastated, holocaust higher than Hiroshima,
Result of the untested first, having known;
Still it was thrown,
World War II brought to close,
The Allies had won,
Brought Nazi Germany to its feet!
Atom Bombs had won the war,
Call it the ugly face of science,
That brought peace for time!

Ceasing war that shook the World,
The subservient served for good;
Ceasefire, surrender, Hitler finished,
"Hitler moustaches" much in fashion,
The sign flourishing in British India!
Little could "The British" do!
Well before 1947, a Country to be born,
"Babus" the British loved calling Indians,
Working in offices under them,
Bore Hitler-cut moustaches, toothbrush like;
Style to adjust the gas mask,

To avoid mustard-gas attack!

World developed and progressed thou',
Wars have but continued for good,
Threat of going nuclear looms large,
Type and intensity several notches up,
UNO, Security Council belittled now and then,
Veto power plays its role!
World silently waiting for an evil force,
Could unleash and finish it, one day!

Force unleashed, off and on, suppressed,
Could not leave images into oblivion,
Many years since Hitler killed himself,
Many more have been reborn,
Some sort of suppression is healthy and necessary,
Worry of those threatening a nuclear holocaust,
Keeps the World on the edge,
As nuclear threat continues to date!

Lessons from history must be learnt,
Before it gets too late,
History seems repeating itself,
Turmoil continues unabated,
It's Moscow versus Kyiv now,
One-upmanship continues,
It's Yesterday Once More!
Need to retrace steps,
Third World War never again!
It's Yesterday Once More,
Never, never, never again!

28
Agonizing Victories

Agony and Victory,
Two sides of a coin,
Connection exists between the two,
Inseparable from each other,
Can't have one without the other;
So intimate with each other,
Unattainable all alone!

If agony is in mind,
Be victorious, have agonies to see;
Makes one think again;
For the follies in victories,
Committed more often than in defeat,
The character in man evokes,
Inhumane character in man;
The animal in man comes outright,
For might is right.

Reason to attain and conquer,
An error, must we understand;
For everything is left behind,
Agony and victory, inseparable they are;
Victory associates agonies,
Call it agonizing victories!

29

The Capital City We Live In

Who has hit the city, neither of us?
But, those at the helm for years, with vested interests;
Caused rampant growth, got out of control;
Others silently watched its decay, responsible too?
A concrete jungle, now a dead city!
Temperatures soaring as never before!

The Capital City, sufferings of residents so profuse;
In confluence with cities all around,
Cos of haphazard growth;
Forming an "Enclave" with cities about;
Habitation thru' and thru', no gaps in between;
Chaotic, abnormal, illogical its growth been;
Spread over fourteen hundred kilometers,
Competence of its planners, indecisive they have been!

Being a Capital City, must it only grow?
There need be limits for its growth,
Else create and be a cause of chaos!
How could the expectations grow as wild as this?
Is it normal or abnormal growth?
What are the reasons of its growth?
How much area is it of the Nation?
Is it the only city that must grow?

Already crammed, why let others in;
Adding close to a million per year,
Can it afford to take any more?
Vultures out there use freebies to lure influx;
Other considerations directing its growth!

The state of the huge river, Yamuna, sacred it's been;
On the banks of which the city has been!
Its status reduces to a sewer, in the lean days;
Sustains no aquatic life, no remorse;
Now much across it, the city has over grown.

Why the hell is it growing further?
Horizontal spread no more, begins vertical now;
Fill up yours; let some slip in mine;
Respecting mutual growth, began growing on its own?
Interested parties letting it outgrow!

Limits to sustain life at its zenith,
Two storey flats to four, now many more;
Dangerous to be in Seismic Zone IV,
Study said so some thirty years ago!
Skyscrapers coming up fast, challenges ahead;
Not afraid of despite warnings declared years ago!

Brimming up with vehicles all over,
Collecting taxes, profitable to the state;
Parking facilities insufficient, lined up on the roads;
Chaotic traffic flows, accidents many more;
No worry as 'trauma centers' coming up fast!

Are we really proud of the fact?

"Labeled the most polluted city in the World",
Unburden it; take the factories off;
Banished by the Courts long ago?
Forgotten, waiting for revised orders!

Claimed to be the greenest city, with lot many trees;
Overgrown trees, posing problem in plenty!
Many diseased, to be pruned, staying on their own;
Care selective, work selective, working willfully unburdened;
Buildings built, now demolished, over and again;
No time to check, if stayed its lifetime;
Shear lust to make more, big time money at stake;
Got them down much before time!
Debris unclaimed, never part of soil again!

What a trash made of structures so perfect!
Unusable to build structures, the glue effect lost; They knew
its plight, not keen to act right;
Effective building bye-laws, failure to implement; Forget
knowing all they should, future not in mind; Laws to save
environment, keep it clean and right; Never thought of,
except pure expansion for sure;
Enjoy financial gains, heavens take care of else!
From a green, less developed in 1950's;
Concrete jungle, its new glory!
Check population census, things already gone awry;
Travesty of facts, new problems after independence;
Chanakyapuri in New Delhi built then, still going strong;
Thought and planning so perfect,
After a century, still open enough, lively and perfect;
An area about five miles in circle, place most livable!

Other places developed much later,
Dungeons created, filth everywhere;
Mountains of filth surround all over!
Difficult for those, seeing city inching to its slow death;
Now in nineties, pray all those at the helm;
Take decisions, still time, before it gets out of hand!

Four lakhs at the beginning of twentieth century,
Grew four times by 1947, year of independence;
At three crores today, a frightful figure today;
Seventy five times it grew in just over a century!

Consider it part of your motherland,
How much more could it take, well beyond limits, its land?
Tentacles of growth, its decay spreads all around;
Engulfed villages within, vacuoles created;
Serve as in cells, as dumping ground of wastes!

Bubble of growth has reached its zenith,
Liable to burst someday, not far away;
Population density over 30000 per square mile,
One of the highest in the World,
Need know anymore, to know its state of health;
One looks and says, "It's like a mega slum!"

Pointing anticipated miseries, better in many ways;
Gives time to act, mitigate them, only if wishing to;
Selectively see; selectively hear, hardly any problem;
Won't it be right, look, hear, do only right;
Hook it out of its deadlock, carve its future right;
Let it stay bright and prosperous,
Is right in your hands!

30

Much to Recover

Aśoka the Great, of Mauryan Dynasty!
So named by his mother, her sorrows he removed;
Strong Emperor, ruthless against looters;
Thus, lives Aśoka through Edicts.

Memories erased; the history lost for two millenniums,
A British engineer discovered Edicts in 1915,
Beloved of the Gods – Devanampriya!
Priyadarshi–affection, regards for all!

Bindusar his father, Chandragupt his grand;
Lineage so famous, extended boundaries far and wide;
Kalinga War proved his nemesis!
Killed a lakh, found solace in Buddhism!

Sorrow for annexing, arose "Law of Piety";
Pious King remembered for his deeds,
Details from inscriptions on Edicts,
A Great, ideal King, ruled 268-232 BCE.

Thus, lives Aśoka through Edicts, his glory lives on!
Shining star, the brightest amongst Monarchs!
Aśoka's Creation, the State Emblem of India!
Lion of Sarnath, a modified emblem!

"Satyamev-Jayate", victory of truth!
Moto from Upanishads, below its Emblem;
Thus modified, Dinanath its creator;
Maintains copyright, modifies to glory!

Shanti Niketan the Alma mater, Emblem he created;
Four Asiatic lions, base circular;
Power, courage, pride, confidence, represents;
As the Lion look all around, on alert;
Brilliant in its completion, historical glorification!

Glorious is the history, glorious its sayings;
Relics in plenty being restored for sure,
Much we say, we have in texts;
Much that we do need be virtuous!

Our Nation, a land of Rivers;
Holiest of the Holy, Ganga and Yamuna!
Mother to a billion, blessings do they seek!
Blessed is Yamuna where Krishn played his flute!

Flowing waters were pure, for a while;
Purifies the soul, of one and all;
A Holy dip refreshes all, a belief!
Sit back, think, what we do!

Still one of the most polluted amongst rivers;
Hazardous loads in, shouldn't be;
Lifeless in stretches, insensitive we've been;
With the man on the rock, in the pandemic recently;
Fresh and clean were the rivers, nature shows the way!

Yes, holy are the rivers,
Praying! As Goddesses!
Is it all to do, continue to do?
Is it enough that we can do?

Rivers we pollute remain unclean,
Clean its water, for daily use;
Boil it; clean it, and then do we use;
Holy are the rivers, unholy our ways!

The water maligned, year-on-year;
Overloaded with wastes, all along its way;
Some industrial, raw sewage keep discharging in!
In midst of political blame-game, diplomacies;
It's time to act; much we can do!

The river still stays holy, no remorse;
The beliefs so entrenched amongst all,
Learning's not been followed these days,
Still enjoy a holy dip, should we continue to?

Auspicious days taking holy dip,
Care not for the rest of the lot!
Traffic jams all along, time wasted for long!
Thinking only of the dip!

Traffic stuck on the highways, for hours;
Diverted through the fields, no relief!
Ambulances, urgent movements, must all they wait;
For thousands are there taking a holy dip!

The dip takes the whole day long!
Lanes chock-a-block, drivers asleep on steering;
Traffic controllers shy off, stay away, nothing to say;
While people busy taking the holy dip!

Thoughts must match our deeds,
Teachings practiced as in the scriptures,
Water maligned a created disaster!
Could be holy once again!

With mouths shut, beliefs true, not enough;
Holy rivers must also remain clean,
Beliefs belied, until they get cleaned!
Pray rivers to be cleaned.

History is vital, repeats itself again;
When Aśoka was forgotten, minds got corrupted.
Thousand years of invasion, natives enslaved!
Experiences enough, now time to change;
A change for the better! Much to recover!

31
Ageing a Perspective

Ageing of life,
Is ageing of vessels!
Of blockages in the vessels,
Ageing of water supply!
Cos of blocked pipes,
Rusting, a reason!

Plaquing of vessels versus rusting in the pipes,
Akin to rusted vessels, plaque in the pipes;
Interchangeable processes, similar in action;
Ends the supply to the man;
It's of blood supply in the man, water supply to man;
End of the function, cellular and cells they thrive in.

Functional disorder with time,
Failure of cleansing processes,
Failing organ function and functioning of the home,
Supply the only reason,
Of the nutrients, and water;
As may be!

Quality of life altered,
Inefficiency to analyse, life time processes;
Prevention is postponing, cleaning it in time;
Repairing is not renewing;

Change of organs, changes of pipes;
Intricate and interdependent problems!

Of water supply versus blood,
Water pipes changeable, bypass with new ones;
Break the walls and change all over,
Stay in alive, change of organs, live a li'l longer;
Costly processes, longevity not assured.

May cost a life and a house;
Require medical help, a team of specialists;
The other engineers, architects and masons!
Makeover, not as efficient!
Life processes affected,
Reduce life times!

32

It's Time to Ponder

Our Citizens, natural and naturalized;
One, with forefather's ever native;
Others, acquired citizenship in the past;
Majority of them true with the land,
Living before invaders looted,
Looted and destroyed the land!

Many were converted, the group alienated;
The majority who fought for their land,
Sacrificing their lives for gaining freedom,
Drove away the then rulers,
Year 1947, independence gained, hard fought it was!

Percentage staying back had motives concealed,
Used the land and worked with a plan,
Continued to be in independent land,
There have been enough traitors in the land,
The trouble makers were and still there!

Then there were those with soft corners,
Represented those working against the land,
Migrated, majority speaking for a cause;
Have vested interest in the land!
Incomprehensive of history critics were,
With li'l interest whatsoever in the land,

Of those settling to improve their prospects,
Settled almost two millennium back,
Accepted, live amicably till date;
Staying and following the norms,
Contribute in the welfare of the land!

But of those having duality of thoughts!
Fanatics and fanaticism, way of teachings;
Huddled with their own,
In the land now not their own,
Living in the land as if their own, not their own!

A section in connivance with other, not their own;
Working for them as if their own,
A leg here and second there,
Maintaining their ends meet in both distinct lands,
Making the best of both,
Working here, living here, and behaving as unowned;
Not our own, to rule our own!

With brother in one and sis' in another,
Live here and marry there,
Status of naturalized citizenship through marriage,
Justifying living self willed,
Relatives created in both!

The land that sheltered them,
Gave them all that it could,
Alas! Allegiance to the very land remains suspect;
Is in the news and newspapers, isn't at all good!
Hence must be true!

Create unrest for the reasons unreasonable,
Why did they not go then?
Political personalities divided them then,
Used them for the best of the motives,
The very fabric learnt from the rulers who ruled.

There are problems faced by the majority,
Newer happenings, newer troubles;
Praying Gods, they have been for generations;
Now reasons to arrest them for creating unrest!

Courts could try them for creating unrest,
Motivated politics behind dirty game,
Who taught them, the misrule so untrue?
Alas, learnt from those who divide to rule!
Divide and rule!

Two hundred years long was the misrule,
Lessons learnt have been bad,
Now ruling through misrule,
To gain power and to rule!

Continue to divide and rule,
But dividing whom have they been,
The majority who fought for their land,
Sacrificing their lives to gain freedom!

Looters of humanity, taught misrule;
A reason unjust, against the majority;
Rules carved to rule!
How about rules to patronize!
Vying one against the other,

Disfavoring the majority!
Secular democracy thus declared in 1976!

Multiplying against logical time,
Trying to have a league, not their own!
Hopeful of further dividing the land,
It's time to nip the evil in the bud,
A saying we must remember!

Land where Ram and Hanuman live till date,
Revered for thousands of years,
Praying deities, a way of life;
Now being used to fight for their rights,
What else could they do!
What's so wrong and what's so bad, if they do!

Very reasonable and logical to do,
Even this being held against the law,
The very fabric of independence in defiance!
It's time to ponder, set things right!

Seventy-five years on, still not too late;
Would they see reasons?
Reasons unreasonable!
Foresee events before it gets late,
Too late, too late!
It's time to ponder!

33

Heartfelt Remembrances

As Covid pandemic creates havoc,
Problems pervading all over,
As destiny begins to roll,
No home left unaffected,
Ailment taking its toll!

Our homes not bereft of problems,
Discreetly got affected,
Three sisters left one after another,
Over less than one year plus half,
Heart and Soul of three house-holds,
Left after finishing their lives!

Finishing off the times they lived,
Changed life in three households forever,
Most caring and loving threesome,
The families and others they cared,
Such was the life they lived!

Think of great upbringing they had,
Most dutiful towards one and all,
Left for heavenly abode,
For sure only one thing is certain,
Person is born, grows, and then goes!

Where do they go? Why should they go?
What is that that leaves and goes?
The Soul that goes, ageless it is;
Lord Krishn says it leaves the body,
Changes its clothes, enters a new one!

The cycle of rebirth then switches off,
Attains 'Moksha', Soul stays in heaven,
A rebirth is ordained, if wishes left unfulfilled,
A concept, good to believe;
Make one, live on in belief!

The qualities in the person, remembered;
Bereft of close one, remembrances live on;
As they continue to live within us,
Reasons let thinking to continue,
Of the times gone by,
Unfinished work must continue!

For all of us, now
Remember, mother and the two sisters;
Beautiful things that they taught,
Making lives peaceful and good,
For their thoughts for sure,
Will carve the future of all,
The members left behind,
And remember beautiful times spent!

34

Relatively Speaking

Relatively speaking,
A half foot forward,
A foot supporting from hind, behind;
Relative position at the instance,
Maintains balance,
In relation to a constant,
Personality emanates!

Philosophically or in science,
Every truth is also relative,
Dark one side, bright the other;
Facts continue to revolve,
Some inside, a bit outside;
Maintains its balance!
Personality personified!
Relatively speaking!

35
Difficult Times

Extremism and Barbarism,
Barbaric itself an act so brutal,
Savage, inhuman & Neanderthal,
Inflicts sufferings so extreme,
When survival get remote,
Life becomes a burden.

Extremism is negative and perverse,
View against, accepted universally,
Would they act this time, in time?
Consider unsocial activities as normal,
Definition of normalcy so perverse,
Stone-age life, in modern World!

Still acceptable to many,
Masquerading in civil societies,
Popping up on idiot-box off and on,
Diseased mind, require resetting;
Social isolation only way,
Such leaders ought to be shunned.

The World need to unite,
Cannot go unchecked,
How so long it may take?
The rebels need to be managed,

Isolated, taken care captivated,
Time to act now!

Done by extremists,
Is the World united?
Not seemingly so,
Nation with no technological support,
Possess weapons of the best of the armies,
It's like back in medieval times!

With dresses and arms,
Matching the elite forces in the World,
Many forces may even not have,
Few are keen to let it happen.
Aided by the like minded group of nations!

Nations supporting, stand identified;
Are culpable of genocide,
For without support and state sponsors,
Highly improbable to have gone this far,
Countries need to act fast,
Stop barbarism going on,
Help when it must, it should!

Nothing seems happening presently,
Silently watching the upheavals,
All that is happening for now,
Views supportive from like minded,
Unfortunate, savagely and unacceptable!

Such groups now being identified,
Above law, can't happen for long,

Forcing outrageous acts to hapless and weak,
One runs into another,
Switching between barbarism and extremism!

Extremists become barbaric,
Barbarians are extremists perverse,
Have no human concerns,
Like a tiger on a lamb,
Committed by humans, acts so grisly!
Intolerable views, wholly unacceptable!

For an animal has limited thoughts,
Human extremists do with full knowledge,
One act two words, barbarism and extremism,
Enforcement the keyword,
Take away the freedom, demeanor of a beast,
Acts, ominous to its people all over!

To take it away for self found views,
Suppression of feelings, crime against humanity;
Feeling is sign of life in World,
Seen amongst most living beings,
Even carnivores don't kill without a reason,
It is treason against humanity!

For humans with all sensibilities,
Barbarism and extremism, inexcusable;
What right has anyone?
So inhuman to be,
Existing laws and systems prove ineffective.
Time and again, over and over again,
Do it now, do it now!

Mouths shut, nibs broken;
Human rights under threat! Why look the other way?
Wind of change left forlorn,
Where are they? When would they say?
Say where they need not, all that they do;
Time to open up, countries need to unite now!

Working for a reason,
Quiet when they shouldn't
Activists stay silent, right across the world;
No courage to speak,
For no personal or political gains!

'Jayasi', legendary Sufi Poet unfolds,
More than two centuries later in 1540 CE,
Of Rani Padmavati of Chittorgarh,
And the brave twenty-thousand!
Jumped in burning pyre,
Saving their honor and torture from Khilji,
The tyrannical predecessor of the land in question!
'Sati' it was, horrific truth of the times!

Irony of fate of millions hangs in balance,
History rarely changes, repeats itself,
Same mistakes, failure of upbringing;
For the so-called developed World, kept lying low!

Numero uno amongst Nations, the World rallies around!
Mission over, left the weak to fend;
Armed to tooth, a nation destroyed, reprehensible;
Arms mafia after all control all acts!

36

Dealing Emergencies for Free

Need based is an emergency,
Urgency to seek corrections,
Health imperfect, an emergency;
To be done for free!

Well said, 'Where else could it be free?'
Won't mind, if applied to all;
All services may be emergent,
Can all be for free?

Ongoing cases in the Courts,
Seeking justice, also emergent in nature;
All hell break lose when charged for quality service,
A financial breakdown looms large;
Survival in bargain!

Story of a thirsty crow, an emergency it was;
Would die for want of water,
Added pebbles to increase water level,
Quenches his thirst!

Water scarcity, dying for water;
Not unusual in deserts,
Need water from anywhere,
Most dire emergency!

Quenching thirst foremost, an emergency;
Request water-can for free,
An emergency after all!
Few may have no money to pay!
Should it be snatched, if not for free!

Seems like Ram Rajya!
Even non-believers asking services for free,
Even enforcing a few for free,
An adage, 'Nothing is for free',
There is a cost for everything!

Enough of 'Robin hoods' in the land,
Declare services to be for free,
From haves to have-nots,
From very wealthy to very poor,
Hope to get them for free!

Distributors have vested interests,
Vote banks in mind, elections around the corner;
Impose treatment in an emergency,
To be available for free!

The needy move to a state,
Where service is forced to be given for free,
Salute the rulers, so good to their subjects!
Apparent Robin-hoods!

Unfair to ask medical services for free,
In comparison in Western world, it's almost for free;
Still Medical world conveniently targeted,
Seek for self-help their glory!

All other services chargeable,
Not less uncontrolled,
Lawyers fee sky high,
Exorbitant to say the least!

Private hospitals to provide free beds,
Do high profile advocates also provide it for free?
To a percentage of poor, it's essential to be free;
Legal cases, potential to create health issues!

Now forced to seek medical help,
Health issues created by the rest,
Provide services for free! Keep eyes open,
Who can't see, as the needy exist all over?
All services, to all, to be for free!

www.ingramcontent.com/pod-product-compliance
Lightning Source LLC
LaVergne TN
LVHW061618070526
838199LV00078B/7330
* 9 7 8 9 3 6 4 5 2 4 1 8 6 *